# The Cobblestone & The Common

## A Field Guide to the English Spirit of Place

by R·H· Mason

The Cobblestone & The Common: A Field Guide to the
English Spirit of Place
by R.H. Mason
ISBN: 9781989647837
First published October 15, 2025
Toronto, Ontario

Publisher: The Evergreen Centre

Publisher's Cataloging-in-Publication Data
Mason, R.H.
The Cobblestone & The Common: A Field Guide to the
English Spirit of Place / R.H. Mason. – First edition.

Summary: This concise volume, part of the Applied Vernacular
Series, serves as a field guide to the enduring English spirit of
place, decoding the built environment of towns and villages.
It asserts that English history is a vital, living archive worth
preserving, rooted in the applied wisdom of the working
class and characterized by "defiant permanence". The work
analyzes the built vernacular—from timber framing and
Cotswold stone to thatch and dry stone walls—examining how
key social pillars, including the Parish Church, the Pub, and
the Common, function as the Heartbeat of the Common and
the source of local self-sovereignty. By honoring the Quiet
Craft tradition (Stonemason, Thatcher, Wheelwright), the
guide offers an irreplaceable code for human endurance and
resilience.

Identifiers: ISBN 9781989647837

Subjects: Architecture, Vernacular. | Villages—England—History.
| Cultural Geography. | Local History. | Social History. | Great
Britain—Civilization.

Classification: 720.942–dc23

# The Cobblestone & The Common

## A Field Guide to the English Spirit of Place

by R.H. Mason

CHAPTECH SERIES

APPLIED VERNACULAR

A Note on the Series: Applied Vernacular

Welcome to the Chaptech / Applied Vernacular Series.

Chaptech / Applied Vernacular is the art of small, humble books that make knowledge tangible, practical, and joyfully human. Born from the earnest spirit of 1970s scout manuals, National Park pamphlets, mimeographed guides, and the enduring wisdom of the Appropriate Technology Library, this series champions the book as a talisman—a compact, personal artifact designed for engagement, not consumption. We celebrate line drawings that verge on the naïve, the charm of deliberately imperfect diagrams, and the sacred, tactile nature of hand-assembled care. This is instruction as intimacy, expertise as invitation, and the small book as a gateway to doing, making, and discovering.

In a world brimming with fleeting, disembodied information, this collection stands as a quiet testament to enduring knowledge—the kind learned by hand, observed with patience, and proven by practice. Each book is a cultural pocket oratory: an invitation to quiet contemplation and a "first experiment" into a specific facet of the natural world, cultural archives, or practical craft. We celebrate the Applied Vernacular: the language of hands-on wisdom, rooted in everyday experience and the ingenious solutions found in local living. These aren't exhaustive encyclopedias; they are humble field notes, concise guides designed to spark curiosity and equip you with foundational skills and uncommon insights. If the spark catches, resources abound. This is a first step. The journey is long.

This volume, The Cobblestone and the Common, extends the "field guide" concept to the realm of historic wandering, cultural reclamation, and understanding the physical remnants of an essential human experiment in living. It treats the villages and towns of England as embodiments of culture and will and built attempts to create harmonious, purposeful lives—each byways and hedgerow and commons is a hidden structure waiting to be mapped, understood, and re-aligned to an internal map of the soul.

Carry this book with you. Let it be the small weight that anchors your attention, a portable point of reflection. Let it get dog-eared, stained by soil, or marked with your own insights. Use it to deepen your connection to the world around you, to cultivate a quiet competence, and to rediscover the profound satisfaction that comes from knowledge in hand, and practice in heart.

# TABLE OF CONTENTS

# Introduction: The Enduring Tapestry
Wandering through 'Merry Olde England'

Welcome to the journey. This volume invites you to step across the threshold of the familiar and wander through what the collective imagination calls "Merry Olde England.". This phrase represents a romanticized and idealized depiction of England, often associated with cultural richness and an idyllic way of life. Our guide is an invitation to slow down, to notice, and to experience the spirit of a place built not in a single era, but accreted over centuries of human life.

Our journey will take us through the small, humble spaces—the towns and villages—that are the very heart of the English spirit. These communities are defined by human scale and continuous history. We will be field naturalists of the built environment, documenting the patterns left by time.

We'll wander down the narrow, winding lanes of a place like Lavenham, Suffolk, where the sheer scale of the half-timbered Weavers' Houses speaks to the immense medieval wealth of the wool trade, not merely quaintness. These structures are not relics; they are documents of economic history written in plaster and oak. We will pause in the market square of Chipping Campden, Gloucestershire, where the 17th-century Market Hall still stands—a practical, open shelter built not for ceremony, but for the hard-won work of trade and the gathering of communities.

Notice the towering presence of a Norman parish church, or the disciplined, unified harmony of a Georgian terrace in Bath. Each stone, whether roughly hewn or precisely dressed, offers evidence of persistent human craft and deep historical layers. These places are not relics behind glass; they are unique tapestries woven from history, architecture, and enduring culture. They are the practical foundation of a nation, and we

1

treat them as such: a physical, tangible guide to where people live, make, and belong.

## The Enduring Tapestry: Affirming the Living Archive

The image of "Merry Olde England" is a powerful, persistent ideal—often honey-tinted by nostalgia and literature. This book asserts that English history is not a museum exhibit, but a vital, living archive worth preserving and understanding in toto. The work of this guide is to use the lens of the vernacular—the language of hands-on, everyday wisdom—to celebrate this living history.

The charming village is also a complex archive of class, industry, economic change, and the constant friction between preserving the past and embracing the future. We look at a timber-framed house not merely as a beautiful sight, but as a vernacular solution to building with local materials. We examine a village common not just as a green space, but as a historical testament to shared resources and communal rights. Above all, we honor the resilience embedded in these structures, which are characterized by their "defiant permanence" against the fleeting trends of fashion.

We will explore key questions that root us in the spirit of place:

• How has the built environment evolved to reflect changes in social life, from the density of a medieval market to the order of a Georgian terrace?

• What role do local customs—the seasonal festivals, the folklore, the pub rituals—play in shaping the identity and binding a community together?

• How do these communities navigate the challenge of preserving their unique character against the pressures of tourism, modern development, and economic change?

By looking beyond the simple charm, we unlock the powerful, complex stories these stones and beams tell about the people who called them home. This book is an invitation to listen deeply to these places, to see the evolution in the architecture, and to discover the enduring, assertive power of the past in the present. This defiant continuity is inspiring, proving that a place can evolve, endure, and remain recognizably "home" for generations

# Chapter 1: The Anatomy of Place

## Stone & Timber: A Primer on the Built Vernacular

To understand the spirit of place is, fundamentally, to understand the vernacular architecture—the language of construction rooted in local geography, climate, and immediate necessity. This is not the architecture of courts or academies; it is the applied wisdom of the working class, a practical, resourceful tradition that asserts its own defiant permanence against the fleeting trends of fashion.

The primary materials of the English village are stone and timber, and they operate as a direct geological and biological cross-section of the landscape. They are a declaration of where the materials could be found and the labor performed.

Where the great English forests thrived, timber framing became the dominant form. This is architecture stripped to its structural DNA: a robust skeleton of great oak posts and beams, filled in with non-structural panels of wattle and daub (woven laths coated in clay).

This exposed, half-timbered style, seen in places like the great cloth halls of Lavenham, is an honest structural statement. The construction reveals the sheer strength and skill required to shape the massive oak frames. The timber-framed house is an economic and structural masterpiece, a testament to the fact that early wealth and sophistication were often measured in the density and complexity of one's wooden skeleton.

# THE PERMANENCE OF STONE

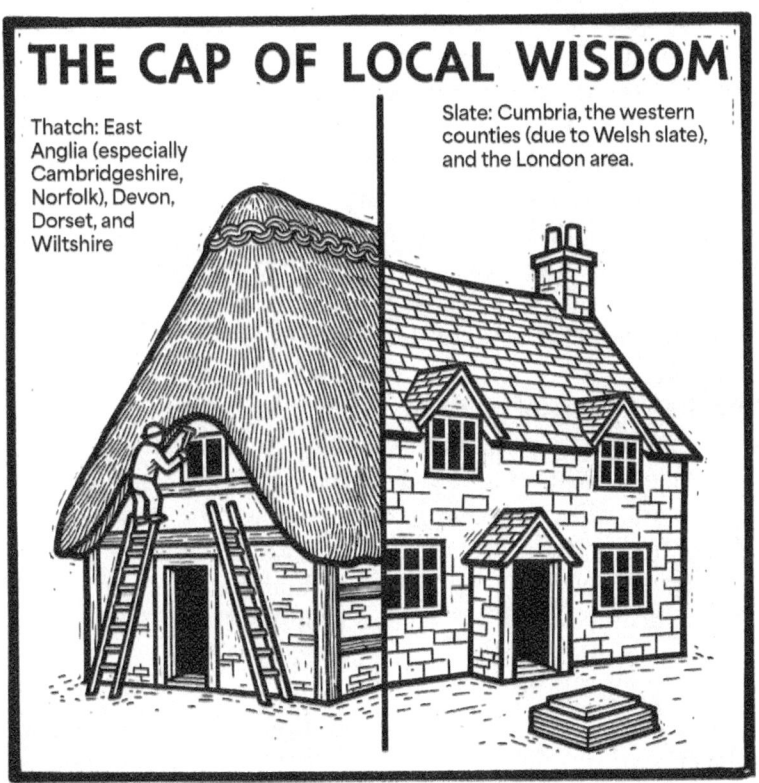

# THE CAP OF LOCAL WISDOM

Thatch: East Anglia (especially Cambridgeshire, Norfolk), Devon, Dorset, and Wiltshire

Slate: Cumbria, the western counties (due to Welsh slate), and the London area.

## The Permanence of Stone: The Limestone Belt

Move westward and northward, and the language changes entirely. In regions like the Cotswolds, Yorkshire, and parts of Cornwall, the bedrock asserts itself. Here, architecture is defined by permanence and integration with the landscape.

The vernacular stone house is not built on the landscape but of it. Look at the honey-coloured houses of the Cotswolds: they are made from the local limestone, quarried nearby, dressed into manageable blocks, and stacked. Their beauty lies not in ornamentation, but in the material's integrity and ability to weather perfectly, melding into the hills from which they were cut. The same intelligence is found in the dry stone walls that stitch together the fields of the Peak District and Yorkshire Dales. These walls, built without mortar, rely on gravity and precise fit—a testament to applied craft that requires generations of accumulated knowledge.

## The Permanence of Stone: The Limestone Belt

Completing the anatomy of place are the vernacular roofing materials, which further assert regional identity. Thatch (in East Anglia, the South Coast) is an ancient, insulating material that demands high, steep roof pitches and skilled, often hereditary, craftspeople. Conversely, Stone Slabs (Cotswolds, the North) required a structural ingenuity where tiles were thickest and heaviest at the eaves, gradually slimming towards the ridge—a sophisticated structural gradient dictated entirely by the physics of the material.

The vernacular home, from its stone foundation to its cap, is thus a concise answer to a complex set of regional problems: What resources do I have? What climate must I endure? What function must this building serve? These structures are not quaint; they are defiant monuments to regional intelligence.

## The Permanence of Stone: The Limestone Belt

The architecture of the English town and village is a continuous, defiant narrative written in stone and mortar. Every structural change, every new style layered upon the old, is a response to a specific problem, an expression of a new social innovation, or a silent memorial to a transformative event. By learning to read these changes, we decode the economic and cultural history of the people who shaped them.

## Medieval: The Problem of Survival and the Innovation of Density

The medieval period (c. 1100–1485) was defined by the urgent problems of defense, market function, and density. Architecture served immediate, practical needs.

- **Problem:** Maximizing utility on constricted urban plots, often dictated by tax boundaries.
- **Innovation:** Jettying (overhanging upper floors) in timber-framed construction. This allowed builders to expand the functional living space above the narrow footprint of the expensive burgage plot, sometimes legally circumventing ground-level property tax assessments. This practical maneuver reveals the relentless pressures of medieval urban economics and space management.
- **People and Events:** The Wool Trade and the Black Death. The immense wealth generated by the trade funded the grandest parish churches and civic structures. Post-Plague labor shortages paradoxically empowered the surviving artisan class, leading to a rise in the status of the common person and the construction of more permanent, higher-quality yeoman farmsteads.

## Georgian: The Problem of Chaos and the Innovation of Order

The eighteenth century (Georgian era) reacted against the perceived chaos and lack of hygiene of the medieval streetscape. The ruling problem was establishing civic order, sanitation, and refinement.

- **Solution:** The importation of Classical ideals—symmetry, proportion, and regularity—from the Continent. This led to the widespread adoption of the Georgian terrace and the uniform street façade. The individual was subdued in favor of the aesthetic and civic whole.
- **Innovation: The Sash Window.** This simple change replaced the small, leaded panes of the past. The large, vertically sliding sashes allowed light and air to flood the interior, addressing sanitation problems and reflecting a new cultural focus on refinement and the domestic interior.
- **People and Events: The Rise of the Gentry and Urban Planning.** The prosperity of landowners and merchants drove speculative development. Places like Bath or parts of Bristol were entirely recast as unified, planned environments, celebrating the collective wealth and rational thinking of the Enlightenment through the creation of squares, crescents, and regular street grids.

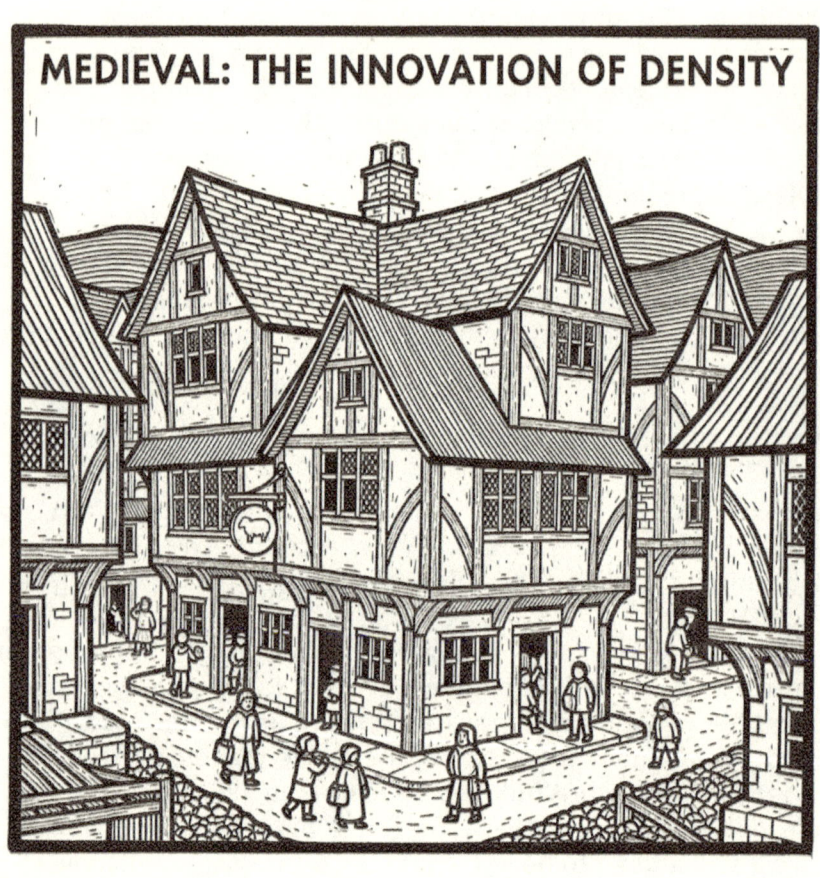

MEDIEVAL: THE INNOVATION OF DENSITY

GEORGIAN: THE INNOVATION OF ORDER

**VICTORIAN VILLAGE: ORNAMENT & NATIONHOOD**

## Victorian: The Problem of Industrial Scale and the Innovation of Mass Production

The Victorian era (c. 1837–1901) confronted the brutal reality of the Industrial Revolution: massive, rapid population growth and the need for durable, cheap housing for a new urban working class.

- **Problem:** Housing thousands of factory workers quickly and affordably.
- **Solution: The Terraced House.** Built of hard-wearing brick (often fired by coal transported via the new rail network), the terrace was the ultimate expression of efficiency and utility. It solved the problem of housing density at scale.
- **Innovation: Ornamentation and Ironwork.** Despite the functional simplicity, the Victorians applied mass-produced ornamentation (decorative bargeboards, ornate tilework, cast-iron railings). This attempted to imbue dignity and individuality into what were essentially standardized dwellings, reflecting the era's democratic but often hypocritical obsession with domestic respectability.
- **People and Events: The Arrival of the Railway.** The new transportation network allowed materials like Welsh slate and standardized bricks to travel far beyond their local source, fundamentally breaking the vernacular tie between material and immediate geography, yet binding the whole nation closer together through shared architectural fabric.

By tracing the visible evidence of jettied beams, unified Georgian terraces, and mass-produced Victorian brick, we are not looking at static history. We are observing a defiant record of how English people solved their problems—from survival and defense to sanitation and mass housing—and how those solutions shaped the very landscape we wander through today.

## The Defining Characteristics of the English Village

The English village is not merely a settlement; it is the physical manifestation of domesticity, safety, and cultural rootedness. Its unique character is forged by a profound commitment to human scale, a deep reliance on local materials, and a structure that fosters community cohesion—elements that collectively create the powerful sense of "hominess" we recognize.

## Uniqueness and Durability: The Human Scale

The first, and most enduring, characteristic of the English village is its scale. Unlike the often-unfathomable density of the city, the village is built to the measure of a walking person and a shared conversation.

- **The Walking Radius:** The essential components—the church, the pub, the green, and the village store—are typically within a short, manageable walking radius. This isn't merely convenience; it's a structural guarantee of social interaction. Every necessary function requires casual, repeated engagement with one's neighbors, ensuring that community identity is constantly renewed.
- **Organic Growth:** Most villages are not planned according to a fixed grid (like Roman or North American towns), but grew organically around a resource (a spring, a ford, a common field) or a powerful entity (a manor house, a church). This results in winding, often illogical lanes and eccentric property lines that defy modern standardization, reinforcing the sense that the place has simply always been there.
- **The "Huddle" of Safety:** The characteristic clustering of houses around the village centre—the huddle—speaks directly to the historical need for security and mutual defense. This compact arrangement creates sheltered, intimate spaces, fostering a feeling of safety and protection that resonates with our deepest concepts of domestic sanctuary.

The Lasting Pillars: Church, Pub, and Green

The structure of the English village is founded on three essential, enduring pillars that separate it from other types of settlements:

- **The Parish Church**: Often the oldest and most architecturally imposing structure in the village, the church stands as the temporal anchor—a visible record of nearly a thousand years of continuous community life. Even in secular times, its spire or tower serves as a

# THE LASTING PILLARS: CHURCH, PUB, & GREEN

non-negotiable geographical and historical landmark, asserting the village's deep roots.

- **The Village Green (The Common):** The Green is the practical and symbolic heart of the village. It is a historical testament to communal ownership and shared resources, where rights—such as grazing animals or holding markets—were collectively negotiated. It is the democratic core, the stage for local festivals, games, and impromptu gatherings, embodying the spirit of local democracy and shared belonging.

- **The Public House (The Pub):** The Pub is the un-official common room and social exchanger. It is the vital secular space where the hierarchy of the outside world is temporarily suspended, serving as a primary location for gossip, celebration, and the maintenance of local social cohesion. Its permanence reinforces the continuity of the village's daily social life.

## The Essence of Hominess: Why It Is Inspiring

The unique character of the English village is inspiring because it offers a defiant contrast to the modern experience—it champions the local, the lasting, and the tangible.

- **Material Honesty:** As explored in the previous section, the commitment to the local vernacular (stone, timber, thatch) means the village feels inherently honest and of its place. The houses look like they belong, having been literally carved from the surrounding land. This material integrity lends itself to the comforting feeling of permanence.
- **Domestic Sanctuary:** The pervasive sense of enclosure and intricacy— low doorways, small windows, winding paths, and high hedges— cultivates an atmosphere of privacy and sanctuary. It is a world deliberately scaled down and protected, creating the powerful illusion of a timeless, secure retreat from the wider world.
- **The Layered Story:** The villages that endure are those where different eras coexist without erasure. The Georgian frontage is built onto the medieval frame; the Victorian extension connects to the Tudor cottage. The village, therefore, inspires by demonstrating that history is not linear; it is a continuous conversation, proving that a place can evolve, endure, and remain recognizably "home" for generations. It is this defiant continuity that makes the English village an irreplaceable object of contemplation and study.

14

# Chapter 2: The Heartbeat of the Common

## 1. The Parish & The Pub: Community and Shared Space

The social geography of the English village is defined by two structures that stand as competing, yet mutually reliant, poles of community life: the Parish Church and the Public House. They are the twin engines that regulate the spiritual and secular heartbeat of the common, ensuring that collective life continues regardless of state or economic upheaval.

### The Parish: The Anchor of Continuity and the Civic Archive

The church stands as the village's temporal anchor and its greatest architectural inheritance. It is not merely a place of worship; it is the physical memory of the community.

- **Architectural Monument to Longevity:** The village church visually asserts the defiant continuity of the community. Consider St. Mary's Church in Fairford, Gloucestershire. Its glorious, complete set of medieval stained glass survived the Reformation, not because of official decree, but because of dedicated local loyalty and ingenuity. The very preservation of the building's fabric becomes a testament to the village's own will to endure, linking the present day back to the 15th century without a break.

- **The Archive of the People:** Beyond its religious function, the church historically served as the civic center and legal repository. The heavy oak Parish Chest, found in many vestries, was used to store not only sacramental silver but also vital records: the parish poor books, the lists of constables, and the official registers of births, marriages, and burials. The church was, quite literally, the hard drive of the community, where history was recorded, stored, and managed.

- **The Shared Yard and the Grave:** The churchyard functions as the most intimate communal space—the final, quiet common ground. The pattern of gravestones—the elaborate memorials to the gentry near the chancel, the simpler slate stones of the artisans further out—reveals the social structure and economy of the community, visually reinforcing its long-term bonds.

## The Pub: The Engine of Social Exchange and the Hearth of Vernacular

If the church defines the spiritual and historical depth of the village, the pub defines its social velocity and its present, unscripted life. It is the necessary secular counterbalance, embodying the democratic spirit of the village.

- **The Unofficial Common Room:** The Pub operates as the vital third space, distinct from the private home and the formal civic space. It is where the hierarchy of the outside world is temporarily suspended, and genuine local democracy is practiced over a pint. Historically, pubs like The Llandoger Trow in Bristol or countless coaching inns served as the hubs for commerce, land deals, and even local recruiting offices—functioning as the essential site of social cohesion and practical networking.

- **The Architecture of Intimacy (The Snug):** The best village pubs are designed for intimacy. Their low ceilings, small interconnected rooms, and separate areas (like the snug or the tap room) are not accidents of design. They compel casual, close conversation, allowing different social groups—the farmers, the tradesmen, the women—to occupy the same building while maintaining their social boundaries. This architecture focuses energy on the vital human-to-human connection.

- **The Hearth of the Vernacular:** The pub is the enduring symbol of local leisure and, critically, the forum where local knowledge—the Applied Vernacular—was passed down. It was the gathering point for local guilds, the site where the blacksmith, the stone-cutter, and the drover exchanged practical wisdom. The constant hum of conversation, fueled by local ale and a shared fireplace, is the unbroken auditory record of the village's working culture.

By placing these two powerful structures in close proximity, the English village creates a balanced, self-regulating ecosystem: the Church provides the anchor of memory and formal identity, while the Pub provides the dynamic social energy and informal dialogue. Together, they ensure that the heartbeat of the common continues, linking the reverence of the past with the vitality of the present.

## 2. Pathways and Public Domains: The Veins of Village Life

Beyond the iconic church and convivial pub, the very fabric of the English village is defined by its shared thoroughfares and open spaces. These are the arteries and lungs of the community, guiding movement, fostering encounter, and grounding daily life in a landscape shaped by centuries of human interaction and natural contours.

### Pathways and Public Domains: The Veins of Village Life

Beyond the iconic church and convivial pub, the very fabric of the English village is defined by its shared thoroughfares and open spaces. These are the arteries and lungs of the community, guiding movement, fostering encounter, and grounding daily life in a landscape shaped by centuries of human interaction and natural contours.

### Country Roads: The Gentle Approach and the Wider World

The intricate network of country roads, winding lanes, and ancient footpaths that lead into and out of a village are more than mere connectors; they are transition zones, each with its own character, historical purpose, and a distinct rhythm. They snake through fields and hedgerows, setting the pace, preparing the visitor for the intimacy of the village core, and continually reminding residents of the wider, often wilder, world beyond their immediate parish bounds. To navigate them is to engage in a quiet dialogue with centuries of movement and land use.

### A Spectrum of Paths: A Tapestry of Movement

England boasts an intricate and historically layered hierarchy of routes, reflecting the myriad ways people and goods have traversed the landscape for millennia:

1. **Footpaths (Public Rights of Way):** These are the most intimate arteries, for walkers only, granting the public legal access to cross private land along specific, legally protected routes. Far from being neat, paved thoroughfares, they are often mere desire lines, worn smooth by generations of boots, winding through the undulating contours of farmer's fields, or tracing the edge of ancient woodlands. They frequently cut directly through fields of wheat or barley, sometimes via sturdy stiles – steps built into a wall or fence – or simple wooden gates that click shut with a satisfying thud. Crucially, they frequently slice through the dense greenery of hedgerows,

# FOOTPATHS: PUBLIC RIGHTS OF WAY

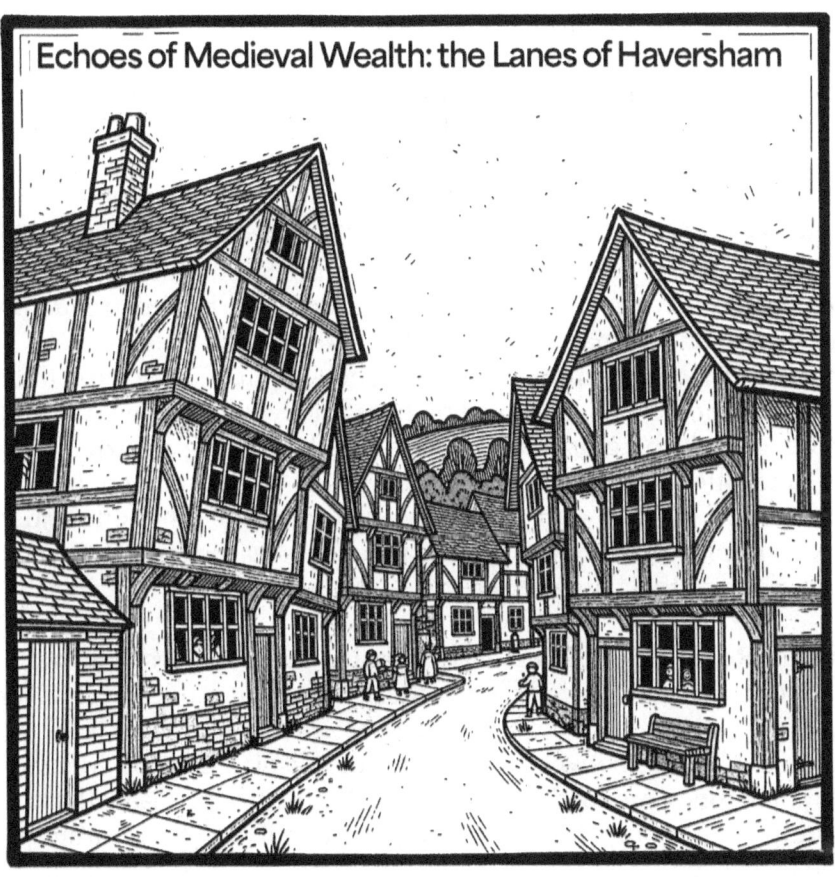
Echoes of Medieval Wealth: the Lanes of Haversham

those living boundaries of hawthorn, blackthorn, and elder, offering unexpected shortcuts, sudden reveals of distant vistas, and a unique, intimate perspective on the working landscape. Imagine the farmer walking his fields, the courting couple on an evening stroll, or the weary traveler taking the most direct route between hamlets, all leaving their imprint on these enduring paths.

2. **Bridleways:** A step up in width and allowance, these public rights of way accommodate not only walkers but also horses and cyclists. Often slightly wider than footpaths, they hint at a past when equestrian travel was far more common for commerce and communication. One can easily picture a farmer on horseback, a drover guiding sheep, or a lady on her mare, all making use of these routes, the ground perhaps churned a little deeper by hooves after a rain shower. They often follow ridge lines or connect villages to larger market towns, allowing a faster, albeit still unhurried, pace of travel than the footpaths.

3. **Byways Open to All Traffic (BOATs):** These are the fascinating, often forgotten, 'green lanes' – historic unsurfaced roads that are legally open to all forms of traffic, including cars, but are frequently so ancient and unmaintained that they are only suitable for 4x4s, horses, or very determined walkers. They might be little more than deeply rutted tracks, canopied by trees, their surfaces a wild mix of mud, gravel, and grass. Driving one feels like taking a journey back in time, often to a period before the internal combustion engine truly dominated the landscape, when the expectation of a smooth, wide road simply didn't exist. They are relics of an earlier age of travel, preserved in their rugged beauty.

4. **Minor Roads (e.g., "B" roads, unclassified lanes):** These are the familiar, often charmingly impractical, routes for modern vehicular traffic, yet they retain the soulful character of their ancient origins as essential links between settlements or to isolated farms. Many familiar "one-lane roads" seen in British films are precisely these, barely wide enough for a single car, twisting like ribbons through the landscape. Their functionality relies entirely on a tacit social contract: the frequent presence of passing places – widened verges, small lay-bys, or even just areas where the hedgerow momentarily recedes – means drivers must anticipate oncoming traffic. A polite flash of headlights, a wave, and one driver will pull over, sometimes reversing a considerable distance, to allow the other to pass. It's a slow dance of courtesy and negotiation, a far cry from the anonymity of a motorway, forcing a connection between strangers that echoes the communal spirit of the villages they serve.

# Echoes of Medieval Wealth: The Narrow Lanes of Lavenham

In places like Lavenham, Suffolk, these minor roads shrink into something even more intimate—narrow, winding lanes that snake through the landscape like secrets half-buried in the earth, their ancient hedgerows brushing the sides of passing cars as if to whisper of forgotten fortunes. Imagine threading your way along one such lane, the tarmac so thin and cracked it yields to the insistent green of encroaching grass, until the first half-timbered facades loom into view, their jettied upper stories overhanging the path like eavesdroppers on a clandestine meeting.

These are no mere cottages of quaint charm; their sheer scale—tall, broad-shouldered structures of oak beams and wattle-and-daub, some three or four stories high—bellows the raw, unapologetic wealth of the medieval wool trade that once made Lavenham the 14th-richest town in England.

Here, in the 15th century, industrious Flemish weavers settled and spun fortunes from the prized "Lavenham Blue" cloth, dyed with woad and exported as far as Russia, filling the coffers of merchants who built these grand Weavers' Houses as both workshops and status symbols. One such tale lingers in the shadow of the infamous Crooked House, erected in 1395 for a prosperous wool magnate; its drunken lean, born of subsiding clay soils beneath the heavy load of prosperity, so captivated imaginations that it's whispered to have inspired the nursery rhyme "There was a Crooked Man."

Yet Lavenham's lanes tell a fuller story of boom and bust: when the once-dominant wool trade faltered in the 16th century, unable to compete with newer textile hubs, the town slipped into genteel poverty. This very decline, however, became its salvation, for its grand houses were untouched by the wrecking ball of "progress," frozen in time like a merchant's ledger left open on a desk. Today, as you emerge from a hidden lane onto Market Place, the sudden reveal of over 300 such timber-framed survivors feels less like arrival and more like stumbling into a chapter of history that the roads themselves have been guarding all along, a silent testament to cycles of prosperity and preservation.

## Ancient Origins, Evolving Surfaces: A Palimpsest of Paths

The enduring character of these country roads and lanes is deeply rooted in their origins. Many, from the humblest footpath to the narrowest car lane, originated as ancient trackways – prehistoric routes following ridge lines, Roman military roads (remarkably straight where possible, but still adapting to terrain), medieval drovers' roads for livestock, or simple paths worn by generations of daily travel between fields and hamlets. Their surfaces tell a story of evolution and practical necessity. Footpaths are predominantly unpaved earth, soft underfoot, often muddy in winter, dusty in summer, connecting directly with the land. Older minor roads might retain a surface of compacted gravel or even just well-trodden earth, particularly in less-used sections, or they may have a very thin, degraded tarmac surface that still feels quite natural and rustic.

However, the more significant minor roads (like many "B" roads) are now typically tarmacked for durability and modern vehicle speeds, yet their inherent narrowness, persistent winding nature, and sharp bends retain the undeniable imprint of their historical character. The act of traversing these roads—whether by foot, horse, or car—means slowing down, observing the hedgerows, noticing the changes in stonework, and engaging with the landscape in a profound way that multi-lane highways simply don't permit. They are not merely conduits; they are part of the enduring tapestry themselves.

## Cobblestone Lanes: History Underfoot, Local Stone, and Diverse Textures

Within the village proper, the change underfoot is often palpable. The rougher earth or tarmac of country roads gives way to the sturdy, uneven texture of cobblestone, sett, or packed earth lanes. These are not merely practical surfaces; they are historical records, reflecting local resources and the slow accumulation of generations.

**Commonality and Cost:** While "cobblestone" (often referring to larger, naturally rounded stones) sounds quaint, more common in many village centres were "setts" – hand-cut, roughly rectangular blocks of local stone. These were durable and provided good grip for horses and carts but were expensive to lay. Their commonality depended on local availability of suitable stone and the wealth of the community. In less prosperous areas, or on less significant lanes, compacted gravel or even just well-trodden earth would have been the norm.

**Local Stone, Local Character:** The type of stone absolutely varied by region, contributing significantly to the village's distinct character.

- **Cotswolds:** Expect golden-hued limestone setts, matching the honey-coloured buildings.
- **Yorkshire/Lancashire:** Darker gritstone or sandstone setts would be prevalent.
- **Cornwall/Devon:** Granite might be used, reflecting the geology.
- **Lake District:** Grey slate or local igneous rocks would feature. These local variations tie the very ground beneath your feet to the surrounding landscape and its building traditions.

**Commons and Paving:** The village common, typically an open grassy area, would not generally be cobbled or paved. It's meant for grazing, recreation, and public assembly, requiring an open, permeable surface. Any paving would usually be limited to paths crossing the common, or around its edges where it meets the High Street or other thoroughfares. Formal village squares, particularly in market towns or planned villages, might indeed be fully paved with setts or flagstones, but the traditional village 'common' is almost universally green.

## 3. The Village Common / Square: The Heartbeat of Shared Life

At the nexus of these pathways often lies the village common or square—the vibrant, beating heart of communal life. Whether a formal paved piazza, a sloping green overlooked by the church and pub, or a less defined open space, this is where public life unfolds.

### The Democratic Forum

Historically, and often still today, the common or square served as the stage for markets, festivals, proclamations, and spontaneous gatherings. It was the primary meeting point, the stage for local celebrations, and the gathering ground for news and gossip. Here, the community's collective spirit was most evident, a living testament to shared existence.

A prime example is **the market square in Chipping Campden, Gloucestershire,** where the 17th-century Market Hall endures as a humble yet enduring symbol of practical communal purpose. Built in 1627 by the town's wealthy wool merchant Sir Baptist Hicks—not for pomp or ceremony, but as a sturdy, open-sided shelter of honey-colored Cotswold stone to shield local women trading butter, cheese, and poultry from the rain—it stands as a no-frills hub for the gritty rhythm of everyday exchange and neighborly mingling. Remarkably,

# HISTORY UNDERFOOT: COBBLESTONE LANES

# HIGH STREET: COMMERCE & CRAFT

this unassuming structure nearly met an undignified end in the 1940s when it was slated for sale to an American buyer, only for the resourceful villagers to rally and outbid the offer with their own hard-earned funds, preserving it as a National Trust gem. To this day, the square buzzes with seasonal markets, but Chipping Campden's flair for the eccentric shines through in its annual Cotswold Olympik Games—revived in 1963 but tracing roots to 1612—featuring delightfully bizarre medieval contests like "shin-kicking," where competitors batter each other's legs in a test of rustic endurance, drawing crowds to the very spot where butter once flew and gossip once swirled.

Further north, **Grasmere Village Green in the Lake District** offers a different archetype of the common. This sloping, often sheep-grazed green, nestled amongst towering fells, is less a formal market square and more an organic space shaped by its dramatic natural surroundings. Its fame is inextricably linked to William Wordsworth, whose family attended the adjacent St. Oswald's Church and whose poetry often drew inspiration from the very landscape visible from the green. Though lacking a grand market hall, it hosts the annual Grasmere Sports, a traditional Lakeland event dating back to 1868, featuring Cumberland & Westmorland wrestling, fell running, and hound trailing—a testament to the enduring bonds of local culture and physical prowess, much like the shin-kicking of the Cotswolds, but adapted to the rugged Cumbrian environment. The green remains a place for quiet contemplation, picnic lunches, and the gentle bustle of visitors drawn by its literary heritage and natural beauty.

In contrast, **Lavenham Market Place in Suffolk** showcases the wealth and civic pride of a prosperous medieval wool town. Dominated by its magnificent 16th-century Guildhall of Corpus Christi, a grand timber-framed building, the market place here is more formalized, a clear statement of economic power. While the Guildhall itself was a centre for trade regulation and civic administration, the open space before it would have teemed with merchants and goods, its very design facilitating commerce. Today, the square still forms the dramatic heart of this remarkably preserved village, drawing the eye to its iconic buildings and reminding visitors of the immense wealth that once flowed through its narrow streets. It continues to host markets and events, living up to its historical role as the central stage for village life.

Architecturally, the common provides an essential breathing space within the density of the village, allowing views of key buildings and framing the natural elements that define the settlement. It's the place where the village announces itself, showcasing its character to residents and visitors alike. In Chipping Campden, the Market Hall anchors the High Street's sweeping curve, its arcaded form echoing the rolling Cotswold hills beyond and inviting the eye to wander from the square's cobbled expanse to the gilded stone facades of merchants' manors, a subtle nod to the town's wool-trading heyday that once made it a medieval powerhouse. Similarly, Grasmere Green opens up breathtaking vistas of the surrounding fells, a natural amphitheatre that visually binds the village to the grandeur of its Lake District setting, while Lavenham's Market Place highlights the architectural mastery of its Guildhall and the timber-framed cottages that define its unique, historic aesthetic.

## 4. The High Street: Commerce, Craft, and Evolving Needs

Flowing through or bordering the common, the High Street serves as the commercial spine of the village. While often modest in scale compared to its urban counterparts, it is the vital hub for goods and services, reflecting the changing needs and economic realities of the community across centuries. More than just a collection of shops, it is a testament to the village's self-sufficiency and its connections to the wider world. Consider the High Street of Chipping Campden, Gloucestershire, a near-perfect example of a medieval wool-trading centre where the broad main street still echoes its mercantile past, lined with golden Cotswold stone buildings. Or the narrower, winding High Street of Shaftesbury, Dorset, which climbs the hill, offering a more intimate yet equally historic commercial experience. These streets are more than just thoroughfares; they are living timelines.

The types of establishments found on a High Street tell a fascinating story of social and economic evolution:

**17th - 18th Century (The Era of Local Craft and Basic Provisions):**
- **The Blacksmith's Forge:** Essential for tools, horseshoeing, and repairs, often with a pungent smell of coal smoke.
- **The Wheelwright's Workshop:** Building and mending carts and wagons, a crucial service for transport and agriculture.
- **The Tallow Chandler:** Producing candles and soap, a ubiquitous necessity before electricity.

- **The Baker:** Offering daily bread, often operating from a stone oven.
- **The General Store / Draper:** A nascent form of department store, selling everything from cloth and ribbons to basic dry goods and perhaps a few imported luxuries.
- **The Inn/Public House:** A place not just for drink, but for lodging, mail coaches, and local business transactions.

## 19th - Early 20th Century (Industrial Revolution's Ripple & Expanding Goods):
- **The Grocer's Shop:** More specialized than the general store, offering packaged goods, tea, sugar, and more diverse foodstuffs, often with scales and a strong aroma of spices.
- **The Butcher:** Dispensing fresh meat, often from locally reared livestock.
- **The Baker & Confectioner:** Expanding beyond basic bread to include cakes, biscuits, and sweets.
- **The Ironmonger:** Selling hardware, tools, and domestic goods, reflecting growing consumerism.
- **The Post Office:** A vital communication hub, often combined with a small shop.
- **The Chemist/Druggist:** Dispensing medicines and early toiletries.
- **The Milliner/Dressmaker:** Providing custom clothing and fashionable hats.
- **The Bank / Friendly Society Office:** Indicating growing financial literacy and organized local savings.

## Late 20th - Early 21st Century (Modern Conveniences and Niche Services):
- **The Convenience Store / Village Shop:** Replacing many specialized grocers, offering a broader, but often less unique, range of everyday essentials.
- **Cafés / Tea Rooms:** Reflecting a shift towards leisure and tourism.
- **Art Galleries / Craft Shops:** Especially in picturesque villages, catering to visitors and local artisans.
- **Estate Agents:** A sign of the housing market's importance.
- **Hairdressers / Barbers:** Enduring personal services.
- **Small Boutiques:** Selling clothing, gifts, or local produce.
- **The Pub (reimagined):** Often becoming more of a gastropub, balancing traditional atmosphere with contemporary dining.

The High Street, in any era, is where the village's pragmatic side meets its social needs. It is where daily life finds its supplies, where gossip is exchanged over a counter, and where the economic pulse of the community is most keenly felt. Its storefronts, often housed in historic buildings, contribute to the distinctive visual identity and enduring charm of the village, making it a physical manifestation of the community's self-reliance and its evolving journey through time.

## 5. Customs and Lore: The Enduring Spirit of Tradition

The true "Englishness" of a village is not found just in its timber-framed aesthetics, roads and various public and private spaces and buildings, but in the survival of its customs and lore—those strange, specific, and often defiant communal rituals that assert a unique identity against the homogeneous tide of the modern world. These traditions are the living heart of the Applied Vernacular, passed down not through books, but through the shared rhythm of action and repetition.

### The Odd and The Quintessentially English

These local practices are unique precisely because they serve no logical modern purpose; they are purely about memory, continuity, and local pride.

- **The Mummers' Play (Winter):** A traditional folk drama, performed primarily around Christmas, that is crude, formulaic, and loud. It features stock characters like Saint George, the Turkish Knight, and a comical doctor who revives the defeated. The sheer simplicity and ritualistic violence of the play (the death and resurrection cycle) is a direct, unbroken link to ancient seasonal pagan observances of death and rebirth. Its power lies entirely in the defiant act of performing the same words and actions, year after year, often in the same pub yard.

- **Wassailing (January):** A specific, often rowdy custom where villagers visit orchards in mid-winter to sing to the apple trees, making noise and pouring cider over the roots. This ritual, notably preserved in places like Carhampton, Somerset, is a literal appeal to the land for a good harvest, chasing away evil spirits. It is a profound, shared affirmation of the village's direct, physical relationship with its primary economic resource: the fruit of the earth.

- **Cheese Rolling at Cooper's Hill (Spring):** The ultimate expression of irrational, local commitment. Every spring in Brockworth, Gloucestershire, contestants risk serious injury to chase a seven-to-nine-pound wheel of Double Gloucester cheese down an incredibly steep hill. This tradition, with no formal governing body, is a testament to the village's right to define its own joy and its own rules—a spectacular act of communal folly that bonds participants and spectators through shared risk and laughter.

## Folklore and The Landscape of Warning

English villages are rich with localized lore—stories that function as both entertainment and as practical morality lessons, often rooted in specific geographical features.

- **Boundary Markers:** The custom of Beating the Bounds—where parishioners walk the boundary of the parish, often striking landmarks with willow switches—is a practical act of legal geography. It ensures everyone, especially the young, physically knows the limits of the community's territory. This is applied geography taught by action.

- **Local Legends:** Every village has its tale of a haunted lane, a phantom hound, or a wise woman. These stories, whether about highwaymen or restless spirits, are not just spooky tales; they are often veiled warnings or explanations for unusual landscape features, passed down to regulate behavior and reinforce the identity of the community against outsiders.

These traditions, from the raw energy of the mummers to the organized chaos of cheese rolling, are the quintessentially "English" elements that defy easy explanation. They are the practical wisdom, joy, and collective memory of a place, ensuring that the past remains perpetually active in the present.

# A FOLKLORE SAMPLER

## Will-o'-the-Wisps
Ghostly Lights and the Warning to Wanderers
Across English marshes and moorlands, glowing lights flicker mysteriously at night—known as will-o'-the-wisps or "fool's fires." Folklore tells that these ethereal flames lure unwary travellers away from safe paths toward danger—bogs, cliffs, or disorienting moors. They serve as spectral warnings, a reminder not to stray too far from the familiar village bounds or safe roads. The persistent tales of will-o'-the-wisp teach respect for the land's hidden perils by turning natural phenomena into folklore guardians of the night.

## The Whispering Lane of East Sussex
In a small village of East Sussex, the "Whispering Path" threads through dark woods where eerie voices seem to murmur with the wind. Folklore recounts warnings carried on that lane's breath—a place to heed or not cross alone at dusk. The whispering voices are said to keep visitors from straying into treacherous marshes nearby. This tale served as a practical guide, teaching generations to respect the dangerous landscape under the guise of ghostly cautionary whisperings.

## The Phantom Hound of Dartmoor
On the wild Dartmoor, tales tell of the Black Dog, a gigantic spectral hound that roams the moorland hills. Its howls foreshadow misfortune and caution travellers to avoid perilous bogs and lonely moorpaths. The village's ghost hound legend encases geological hazards in a memorable moral story. These frightening but compelling warnings keep many from wandering into danger and reinforce communal vigilance over local wilds.

## The Wild Hunt in Cheshire
The Wild Hunt, a spectral chase of ghostly riders through Cheshire's dark woods, forms a legendary motif warning of the boundary between safe village life and untamed wilderness. Villagers told tales of the shadowy hunt to remind themselves of dangers lurking outside the cultivated world. This folklore serves as both a thrilling narrative and a communal boundary marker—guiding behavior, warding off curious wanderers, and binding the community in shared respect for the unknown wild beyond.

# WILL-O'-THE-WISPS:
# GHOSTLY LIGHTS & WARNINGS

# THE WILD HUNT IN CHESHIRE

## 6. The Quiet Craft: Embodied Knowledge and Vernacular Sovereignty

The true, deep character of the English village is preserved not in formal records, but in the quiet, tactile knowledge passed from the seasoned hand to the apprentice. These craft traditions are not merely jobs; they are acts of applied vernacular engineering, where the intimate wisdom of the locale—its stone, its wood, its earth—is translated into the very fabric of daily life. The survival of these skills is the essence of cultural and economic continuity, providing a form of local sovereignty against centralized authority.

### The Engines of Necessity: Sovereignty through Sustenance

These trades occupied the economic heart of the village, ensuring self-sufficiency and transforming raw nature into the essential currency of survival. Their control over resources was a quiet form of power.

- **The Blacksmith: The Engineering Hub:** Operating the forge, the Blacksmith was the village's central problem-solver and the source of applied resilience, maintaining the iron necessary for the agricultural cycle and ensuring the continuity of work. As the supplier of tools and weapons, their loyalty was implicitly tied to the local community, as demonstrated in the Robin Hood myth's "reversal of the guard."

### The Chain of Transformation: The nexus of food and drink established the village's economic sovereignty.

- **The Miller** commanded the natural power of wind or water to grind the community's grain—a literal control over basic nutrition.
- **The Brewer** ensured a safe, necessary drink (ale) for the community.
- **The Baker,** custodian of the communal oven, ensured the consistency of the bread, the community's essential daily food.
- **The Butcher** provided vital protein through skilled slaughtering and curing.

This entire nexus represented the village's ability to extract, process, and control its own vital resources, reducing dependence on external markets or Crown-controlled supply lines.

## The Architects of Place: Defiant Permanence and Embodied Knowledge

These trades ensured the village's defiant permanence, turning local geology and forest into lasting, protective structures. The skill of these artisans was in translating raw matter into cultural endurance.

- **The Stonemason: Master of Geology:** They were the master of local geology, understanding the fault lines, density, and weathering properties of the immediate bedrock to shape the enduring structures of the church and houses. Their skill was in translating raw rock into permanence.

## The Timber Architects:
- **The Carpenter/Joiner** constructed the intricate inner skeleton of the home and created furniture, embodying precision.
- **The Barn Builder's** knowledge of massive cruck frames created towering spaces—the largest structural monument to the agrarian economy.
- **The Thatcher: Applied Physics and Visible Craft:** Mastering the volatile physics of insulation and runoff, the Thatcher capped the structure with a protective layer of local reed or straw, a visible, high-status sign of the roof's fifty-year lifespan—an investment in local time and material. This required specialized, embodied knowledge impossible to acquire from outside the tradition.

## The Wardrobe and Wheel: The Vernacular of Mobility and Personal Durability

These artisans focused on motion, transport, and the durability of personal belongings, facilitating trade and daily comfort—the infrastructure of the vernacular economy.

- **The Wheelwright: Applied Mathematics of Motion:** They were the applied mathematician of motion, constructing carts and wheels using a precise, traditional knowledge of specific woods (dense elm for the hub, flexible ash for the rim) and geometry. Their craft literally kept the village economy moving and connected.
- **Leather and Identity:** The chain beginning with the Tanner's critical, patient process culminated in the Shoemaker/Cordwainer creating durable, bespoke boots—a tangible investment in the physical working life and personal identity of the individual.

- **The Tinker: Resilience through Repair:** The itinerant Tinker represented the final, essential element of resilience, ensuring that all metal, leather, and tin items of the household were kept in constant working order. This culture of repair over replacement underpinned the village's long-term material economy.

## The Custodians of the Land: Applied Ecology and Shared Governance

A resilient village must manage its resources and protect its primary asset: its land and its animals. These crafts involved communal governance and a deep, practical understanding of applied ecology.

- **The Hedgerow Master: Living Architecture:** They were the living architect of the fields, creating impenetrable, long-term, living fences through the highly specialized skill of hedgelaying. This was a patient act of applied ecology, ensuring the long-term health, shelter, and security of the land, simultaneously providing resources and defining boundaries.
- **The Farrier/Veterinary:** Providing essential, immediate care and practical science to the village's economic engine (its working animals and livestock), their skill was critical to preventing disaster and maintaining agrarian output.
- **The Pound Keeper (Hayward):** Local Governance: Serving a vital, communal role, the Pound Keeper managed the common grazing land and impounded stray animals. This position was the direct local enforcement of shared resource management, symbolizing the village's internal ability to govern its own commons without recourse to the Sheriff.

The persistence of these quiet crafts is a profound cultural statement. They are the unwritten encyclopedia of local culture, ensuring that the wisdom of the past remains perpetually active in the hands that shape the present, providing the foundation for the community's moral and economic sovereignty.

HISTORIC COTSWOLDS: THE GOLDEN HEART

# Chapter 3: Case Study 1: The Pastoral Ideal of The Cotswolds

If the English village is a thesis on domesticity and rootedness, the Cotswolds are the perfect, defiant example. This region, spanning parts of six counties, is not a scattering of unique buildings but a unified architectural landscape. It represents the pastoral ideal—a vision of hominess, continuity, and prosperity achieved through an intimate pact between people, geology, and craft.

## The Stone Signature: A Study in Material Honesty

The defining characteristic of a Cotswold village is the Oolitic Limestone—a soft, golden Jurassic stone quarried directly from the subsoil. This geology dictates everything, offering a direct link back to our discussion in

1. **The Honey-Coloured Ideal:** The stone, rich in iron, weathers to a unique, warm "honey colour" that shifts subtly with the daylight. The buildings are not merely built on the land; they are built of the land, emerging seamlessly from the gentle hills. This material honesty eliminates visual dissonance, creating an immediate, pervasive sense of safety and permanence that fulfills the ideal of "hominess."
2. **Applied Vernacular in Stone:** This stone's unique flaking property led to a specific craft solution: Cotswold Stone Slates. These are not thin, factory-cut slates, but heavy, thick slabs of stone. As we noted in our "Quiet Craft" section, these require specific engineering—the slabs are heaviest at the eaves and gradually lighten toward the ridge, demonstrating an acute knowledge of load-bearing physics and material limits, a skill passed down exclusively by stonemasons and roofers.

**Example: Bibury's Arlington Row.** This iconic cluster of former weavers' cottages, built in the 17th century, is a perfect visual lecture on Cotswold vernacular. Their steep roofs and thick walls demonstrate the material-driven solutions to shelter and endurance, standing as an unbroken, tangible link to the region's economic history.

## The Legacy of the Common: Wealth, Church, and Community

The unified aesthetic of the Cotswolds was funded by a specific, historic "event": the immense medieval wealth of the wool trade. This wealth indelibly shaped the community's structural and social core, linking back to our discussion in Chapter 2.

- **Wool Churches (The Civic Anchor):** The colossal grandeur of the village churches in places like Chipping Campden or Northleach defies the small population size of the communities. These are the famous "Wool Churches," built by the patronage of wealthy sheep farmers and cloth merchants. These churches are the ultimate expression of the Parish as the Anchor of Continuity—monuments paid for by commercial prosperity, establishing a legacy of civic pride that was meant to outlast any individual or family fortune.

- **The Human Scale of Daily Life:** This grandiosity is immediately balanced by the Pub. In Broadway, for instance, the imposing Lygon Arms (a historic coaching inn) co-exists with the smaller, more intimate cottages. The village structure itself provides the essential contrast: the magnificent, defiant permanence of the church funded by global trade stands against the human scale of the common stone cottages and the intimate, local chatter exchanged in the pub. This balance between the monumental and the domestic is the essence of the resilient English village.

## Why It Is Lasting and Inspiring

The Cotswolds are the ultimate case study because the region demonstrates a complete, cohesive picture of the English village ideal: Material Integrity: Every structure is a lesson in material honesty, providing the psychological comfort of permanence.

- **Unified History:** The history is legible in the stone: the wealth of the wool trade is visible in the architecture; the skill of the Dry Stone Waller is visible in the fields; and the enduring spirit is visible in the villages that have preserved their fabric for centuries.
- **Domestic Sanctuary:** The gentle, rolling landscape and the uniform, warm stone create an unparalleled sense of domestic sanctuary, fulfilling the deepest human need for a secure, beautiful, and knowable place to call home.

The Cotswolds do not just present an ideal; they present a defiant, enduring lesson in how a community can cohere when its materials, its economy, its craft, and its architecture all speak the same language.

## Action: Tracking the Honey-Coloured Stone (Literature & Film)

The most defiant act of preservation is not physical, but imaginative. The reason the Cotswolds resonate globally — why we feel we "live there even if we never visit" — is that art has successfully translated the region's physical reality (the honey-coloured stone, the winding lanes) into a powerful, portable cultural touchstone.

This imaginative legacy is crucial: it ensures that the ideals of domesticity, permanence, and rootedness are carried forward, empowering the global English-speaking family and diaspora. For those separated by oceans and generations, the image of the Cotswolds functions as a psychological homeland — an uncorrupted vision of origin that art perpetually sustains.

Literary Preservation: The Sensory Record and the Search for Place

Literature provides the foundational, tactile memory of the village, allowing the diaspora to access an inherited culture rooted in a specific place.

- **Laurie Lee's Cider with Rosie:** As the definitive literary anchor, this memoir set in Slad, Gloucestershire, captures the vernacular experience—the taste of the cider, the language, and the intricate life lived within the structures built by the Carpenter/Joiner and the Baker. It is a perfect record of the customs and lore that defined a self-sufficient world, providing the essential cultural substance behind the stone façade.

- **The Romantic Ideal (Betjeman and Macfarlane):** Writers like John Betjeman (with The Shell Guide to England) actively championed the preservation of these villages, documenting them with a reverence that borders on defiant love. More recently, authors like Robert Macfarlane (The Old Ways) have mapped the footpaths and tracks that link these settlements, grounding the spiritual desire for "home" in the physical act of walking the land. The literature validates the inherited memory, proving that the resilience of the Hedgerow Master's work is not just scenery, but heritage.

- **Literary Fiction (P.G. Wodehouse):** Even in the comedies of Wodehouse, the idyllic, often named villages (like Blandings Castle's environs) rely on the Cotswold aesthetic—a benign, protected, and unchanging rural setting—as a counterpoint to the chaos of city life. This established the village as the safe, stable comedic baseline for English domesticity.

# Filmic and Visual Affirmation: The Global Myth of Eternity

Film and television perform the essential task of cementing the visual myth of the Cotswolds globally, ensuring its aesthetic becomes the international shorthand for "timeless England."

- **Period Drama as Cultural Export:** The BBC's continuous output of period dramas, especially adaptations of Jane Austen and Agatha Christie (like Pride and Prejudice or Miss Marple), frequently uses Cotswold villages like Lacock, Wiltshire (on the fringe of the Cotswolds, but sharing the aesthetic) to establish an instant sense of historical and moral stability. These scenes ensure that the architecture—the product of the Stonemason and Thatcher—is universally recognized by the diaspora as the visual code for their cultural origin.

- **Global Backlot and Unbreakable Roots:** The consistent visual language of the region makes it the most effective visual vocabulary for permanence. Whether the villages appear in Harry Potter (establishing the sense of an ancient, hidden world) or in modern film (Bridget Jones's Diary), they function as a visual affirmation—a pristine, unchanging image of "home" that transcends national borders. This cinematic legacy affirms that the ideal of stability is real, empowering the diaspora's sense of inherited identity.

- **The Artistic Tradition (The Watercolours):** Before film, artists throughout the 19th and 20th centuries created thousands of detailed watercolours and etchings of the Cotswold scenes. These simple, replicated images cemented the ideal of the "picturesque" village, acting as the first mass-exported visual memory of the region.

By tracking the honey-coloured stone through these diverse artistic vehicles, we realize that the Cotswolds is more than a location; it is a culturally exported ideal of resilience and domestic sanctuary. It is an imaginative space where the lessons of hard-won, honest craft are eternally relevant.

LAKE DISTRICT: UNTAMED SOUL & WHITE LIGH

# Chapter 4: Case Study 2: The Romanticism of The Lake District

If the Cotswolds represent the comfortable, golden ideal of a domesticated English home, the Lake District represents its defiant, untamed soul. This region of rugged mountains, deep valleys (dales), and vast water (meres) did not grow wealthy through easy commerce but was forged by geological violence and a culture of hard-won isolation. Its enduring appeal is not merely architectural; it is rooted in the Romantic movement that elevated its harsh landscape and simple vernacular life to a global, spiritual ideal.

## Geological Defiance: Slate, Granite, and the Need for Light

The Lake District's unique vernacular is dictated by a geology entirely different from the soft Cotswold limestone, creating a distinct aesthetic that ties directly back to Chapter 1: Stone & Timber.

1. **The Dark Material Truth:** The dominant local building material is rough, dark granite and slate. These stones are immensely hard and difficult to cut precisely, resulting in thick, robust walls and a heavy, sombre colour palette. The necessity for local materials means that nearly every structure carries the visual weight of the mountain itself.
2. **The White-Wash Solution (The Applied Vernacular):** The climate here is perpetually damp, cold, and often shrouded in cloud. To combat the darkness and dampness, villages adopted the functional custom of white-washing or lime-washing their stone or rendered walls. This practice, a brilliant piece of Applied Vernacular Engineering, serves two critical purposes: it provides a sacrificial, breathable layer of protection against the incessant rain, and it maximizes the reflection of the meagre daylight, asserting a necessary brightness against the dark, surrounding peaks.

3. **The Master of the Wall:** The essential artisan here is the Dry Stone Waller. The entire landscape is stitched together by miles of walls necessary to control sheep flocks. This craft demands acute patience and skill with the local, often uneven slate and granite, reflecting the region's hard-won spirit of endurance. Example: Hawkshead. This village is a perfect display of the vernacular contrast: dark, heavy slate roofs set against brilliant, light-reflecting white-washed stone walls, creating a striking aesthetic identity forged by climate and material necessity.

## The Social Geography of Isolation and Utility

The architecture of the Lake District reflects a social geography of isolation rather than density. While the Cotswolds clustered around a common green, the Lake District community is often dispersed across a dale, centered on the farmstead and the market town (like Kendal).

1. **The Isolated Farmstead (The Unit of Survival):** The unit of survival here is the independent stone farmstead (or the longhouse), built to be self-sufficient and capable of withstanding fierce weather. The architecture prioritizes utility: thick walls, small, deep-set windows for insulation, and often, the incorporation of a barn or livestock area under the same roof. This reflects the intense demands of the sheep-rearing economy and a culture of resilient individualism.

2. **The Pub: The Lifeline:** In such isolated geography, the Pub (as discussed in Chapter 2) transforms from a social hub into a vital lifeline. In dispersed villages like Grasmere or Chapel Stile, the pub is the guaranteed meeting point, the place where news, collective effort (sheep-shearing, gathering), and local customs and lore are exchanged, reinforcing the necessary bonds of community against the elements.

## The Romantic Invention: The Power of the Untamed

The most lasting and inspiring quality of the Lake District is its cultural transcendence, driven by the Romantic Movement in the early 19th century. Writers fundamentally re-framed the local experience into a universal ideal.

- **Wordsworth and the Sublime:** The poet William Wordsworth (Lyrical Ballads) and the "Lake Poets" did not celebrate the neatness of the Cotswolds; they celebrated the Sublime—the awe-inspiring, sometimes terrifying power of nature.6 They argued that the rough, simple life of the Dales people, working the land, was inherently more noble and spiritually rich than the chaos of the industrializing cities. This act of artistic defiance turned the poverty and isolation of the farmstead into a moral virtue.

- **Beatrix Potter and Domesticity:** The work of Beatrix Potter (who owned and protected vast areas of the Lake District) cemented this ideal in a global, domestic sense. Her stories often feature the simple, traditional stone farmhouses (like Hill Top) and the small, enduring characters of the working landscape. She domesticated the wildness, exporting the aesthetic of the slate roof and the dry stone wall as the ultimate symbol of a secure, simple, and honest home for children worldwide.

The Lake District, therefore, is an inspiration because its architecture is not about wealth, but about endurance. It proves that the defiant spirit of a place can be preserved not just by stone and craft, but by the power of an idea—the Romantic ideal that champions simplicity, nature, and the moral worth of a life hard-won against the untamed wild.

## Action: Reading the Landscape (Wordsworth and Place-Names)

The ultimate "action" the Lake District demands is not touring, but reading. The landscape here functions as the nation's most profound layered text, a document written in stone, water, and linguistics. This is where the English countryside transcends mere beauty and achieves the Sublime—the Burkean ideal of awe-inspiring majesty and terrifying power that demands spiritual, rather than merely aesthetic, attention.

### The Romantic Invention: Elevating the Sublime

The historical import of the Lake District is its cultural transformation, initiated by the Lake Poets, primarily William Wordsworth (1. 1770–1850). Before Wordsworth, mountains were generally feared as ugly, useless, and dangerous obstacles. His defiant act was to re-frame the harshness of the Lake District's granite and slate—the poverty, the isolation, the relentless weather—as a moral and spiritual virtue.

- **The Weight of Nature:** Wordsworth's project, laid out in works like Lyrical Ballads, was to assert that the simple, uncorrupted life of the dalesman, perpetually negotiating the severe landscape, was inherently more noble than the urban chaos of the Industrial Age. He used the landscape's vastness—the high Fells, the dark Meress— as a counter-force to modernity, ensuring the region became the quintessential "English" symbol of untainted nature and enduring human spirit.

- **A New Gravitas:** This poetic intervention imbued the region with lasting gravitas, proving that the highest form of beauty lies not in the softness of the Cotswolds, but in the struggle for survival—the same struggle reflected in the thick, white-washed walls and slate roofs of the severe vernacular architecture.

# Place-Names as an Unwritten Encyclopedia

The most unique and lasting document of the Lake District's history is its linguistic geography. The region's place-names are not arbitrary labels but a direct, audible link to the successive waves of people who worked this land, tying directly back to the practical knowledge of the village trades.

The language of the dales is a time machine, preserving layers of occupation and the precise function of the land:
Place-Name Element
Origin (Historic Event)
Meaning & Vernacular Connection

## Fell (e.g., Scafell)
Old Norse (Viking influence, post-800 AD)
A high, wild mountain pasture. Reveals the sheep-rearing economy and the work of the shepherds and Farriers.

## Thwaite (e.g., Satterthwaite)
Old Norse
A clearing, often created by human effort; a former piece of wild land. Reveals the strenuous work of the early Barn Builders and Hedgerow Masters clearing woodland for agriculture.

## Ghyll (or Gill)
Old Norse
A deep, narrow ravine or stream. A crucial geographical term that speaks to the immediate hydrology and difficulty of travel.

## Mere (or Tarn)
Old English / Old Norse
A large lake (Mere) or a small mountain lake (Tarn). Defines the region's dominant feature and resource.

## Wath
Old Norse
A ford (a place to cross a stream). Reveals the necessity for the Wheelwright and the Shoemaker to create durable goods for constant travel.

**Action: Decoding the Map.** When we stand in the Lake District, the map is a primary historical source. To see a 'Fell' is to see the Viking era's term for the work of pasturing sheep; to see a 'Thwaite' is to see the history of arduous deforestation. This layered linguistic archive ensures that the landscape we are reading carries the entire weight of its human history, making the very act of knowing where you are an act of historical study.

This regional isolation—geographical and linguistic—is what makes the Lake District so quintessentially and uniquely "English": it is a preserved core where the ancient Norse and Old English roots of the modern language, and the rugged, enduring spirit of its people, remain defiantly visible.

Here are twenty Lake District place-names, each with verified etymology and a meaningful connection to historical livelihoods, reflecting Norse, Old English, and Celtic influences.

### 1. Grasmere
Origin: Old English/Norse
Meaning: "Grass Lake." Pasture-rich valley for shepherds, vital meadow for dairy farming.

### 2. Coniston Water
Origin: Old Norse
Meaning: "King's Farm Lake." Linked to royal land tenure, with stewards and land agents marking boundaries.

### 3. Langdale
Origin: Old Norse
Meaning: "Long Valley." Crucial transport route for packhorse drivers and cartwrights.

### 4. Ambleside
Origin: Old Norse
Meaning: "Sandbank pasture." Settlement at river crossing, important for fishermen and bridge builders.

### 5. Loweswater
Origin: Old Norse
Meaning: "Leafy Lake." Forested, supporting woodcutters and charcoal burners.

## 6. Bassenthwaite
Origin: Old Norse
Meaning: "Bastun's Clearing." Area opened by pioneer settlers and forest clearers.

## 7. Keswick
Origin: Old English
Meaning: "Cheese Farm." Centre of dairy culture renowned among cheesemakers and cowherds.

## 8. Rosthwaite
Origin: Old Norse
Meaning: "Reed-bed Clearing." Reed thickets used by thatchers and basket weavers.

## 9. Waberthwaite
Origin: Old Norse
Meaning: "Willow Clearing." Willow-rich area for wattlers and fence makers.

## 10. Borrowdale
Origin: Old Norse
Meaning: "Valley of the Fort." Defended settlement built by stone masons and warriors.

## 11. Buttermere
Origin: Old English
Meaning: "Lake by dairy pastures." Pastoral hub for herdsmen and butter-makers.

## 12. Ullswater
Origin: Old Norse
Meaning: "Ulfr's Lake" or "Lake of Wolves." Site for early settlers, possibly wolf-hunters.

## 13. Brothers Water
Origin: Old Norse
Meaning: "Broad Water" or "Brothers' Water." Linked to legendary drownings, also vital fishing ground.

## 14. Crummock Water
Origin: Brittonic/Norse
Meaning: "Lake of the crooked river." Provides an essential water source for millers and farmers.

### 15. Derwentwater
Origin: Brittonic
Meaning: "Oak River Lake." Riversides with oak stands used by charcoal burners and woodworkers.

### 16. Elterwater
Origin: Old Norse
Meaning: "Swan Lake." Wetlands where wildfowlers and water reed harvesters worked.

### 17. Ennerdale
Origin: Old Norse
Meaning: "Anund's Valley." Pasture valley vital for cattle and sheep farming.

### 18. Glenridding
Origin: Old Norse
Meaning: "Clearing in the valley." A crucial meadow for grazing and haymaking.

### 19. Threlkeld
Origin: Old Norse
Meaning: "Well of the thrall." Water source, suggesting servile labor or monastic use.

### 20. Ravenglass
Origin: Brittonic/Norse
Meaning: "Sand Point." A coastal village, port for traders and salt-workers.

These place-names blend linguistic roots with everyday occupations, mapping both human and natural history onto the Cumbrian landscape.

# Chapter 5. Case Study 3: The Mythic Ground of Sherwood Forest

If the Cotswolds embody enduring domesticity and the Lake District celebrates romanticized nature, Sherwood Forest is about defiant justice and the mythic right to freedom. This region in Nottinghamshire is the sublime ground where narrative power transcends physical geography, defining its settlements—villages like Edwinstowe and towns like Nottingham—as the custodians of the most enduring archetype in English folklore: Robin Hood.

## The Cultural Contradiction: Myth vs. Matter

The sublime power of Sherwood lies in its core contradiction: we carry the image of an eternal, vast, and untamed forest, yet the physical woodland has been radically reduced by centuries of agriculture and industry. The real defiance of this place is not its physical endurance, but the cultural defiance of its legend.

1. **The Shrinking Archive and the Forest Law:** The enduring gravity of the myth is rooted in the harsh, real-world social control imposed by the Forest Law—a legal system established by the Normans to protect royal hunting rights. Key Norman-French terms like 'Vert' (the protective green cover) and 'Venison' (the right to the deer) were instruments of social oppression, highlighting the core injustice: making the King's leisure more important than the commoner's survival. Robin Hood's defiance is therefore a continuous, radical assertion that the community has a moral right to the wild corrective measure.
2. **The Anti-Establishment Anchor:** The myth represents the most enduring English resistance against central authority. The Merry

Men embody the ideal of a social collective operating outside the Parish and the Crown, creating their own moral order. The towns and villages of Nottinghamshire are defined by their proximity to this moral wilderness, serving as the necessary stage where the myth of social justice is perpetually re-enacted.

## Action: The Domestic Fusion and Ritual Reversal

The genius of Sherwood lies in its ability to permanently mash the mythic, the wild, and the domestic into a single, cohesive, and defiant action. This fusion is not a static memory but a living tradition maintained through ritual.

**1. The Ritual of Disguise and Craft**
The core action is disguise, where the domestic and the wild explicitly fuse. To become one of the Merry Men is to adopt the Lincoln Green—a specific colour of homespun, un-dyed wool that represents the quiet, humble colours of the earth and the skill of the local Weaver/Spinner.

- **The Reversal of the Guard:** Through reenactment, the community ritually turns the symbols of the legitimate town hierarchy into instruments of rebellion. The Blacksmith, who usually forges tools for the lawful Sheriff, now forges arrowheads for the Outlaw. The Baker, who provides bread for the town, symbolically provides sustenance for the rebels in the woods. This ritual reversal asserts that the true morality of the community rests with the common craftsman and their honest labour, not the Crown's agent.

- **The Skill of the Yew Bow:** The legendary skill of the Sherwood archer is a direct transfer of the Quiet Craft tradition. The practice of archery in festivals is the physical embodiment of inherited skill, linking modern participants to the precise, practical knowledge of their ancestors required to master the Longbow. The quarterstaff, the chosen weapon of Little John, is the ultimate assertion that simple, found objects and common sense can defeat the high-status weaponry of the knight.

**2. May Day and the Blending of Social Poles**

This domestic/wild mash-up is most potent in the May Day festivities that incorporated the Robin Hood figure. The entire village would participate in bringing the new season's foliage (the 'wild') back into the domesticated spaces of the town square, ritually integrating anarchy with order.

- **Communal Energy:** The accompanying Morris Dances are a chaotic, vigorous expression of communal energy, momentarily replacing the formal order of the church service with the untamed, exuberant spirit of the forest floor. The community's spirit of defiance is released, celebrated, and then safely contained until the next year.

## The Landscape of Lore: Custodians of the Specific

The longevity of the myth is maintained by anchoring the fantastic to specific, tangible vernacular places.

- **The Major Oak:** The Defiant Monument: The single greatest monument is the Major Oak, an immense, ancient tree. It stands as a powerful, sublime symbol of endurance—a defiance against the axes of industry and agriculture. It is a natural architectural wonder, replacing the stone and timber of Norman structures with bark and branch, yet serving as the definitive, immovable proof of the legend.
- **Edwinstowe and the Marital Ideal:** The village of Edwinstowe is the quintessential domestic anchor. It is here, by tradition, that Robin Hood married Maid Marian. The local Church of St Mary, a beautiful, solid Norman structure, becomes the official, named venue for the outlaw's most famous act of submission to social form. This act of localizing the narrative (a Custom and Lore touchstone) turns the mythical marriage into a localized historical fact, making the village the custodian of the legend's romance and domestication.

## Customs and Reenactment: The Living Archive

The most profound affirmation of Sherwood's mythic ground is the communal commitment to physically recreating the past, turning folklore into annual, living history.

**The Robin Hood Festival at the Sherwood Forest National Nature Reserve** is not simple entertainment; it is a communal assertion of local pride and an active transfer of cultural memory by the villages that surround it. Through jousting, storytelling, and practical archery, the community physically manifests the legend, continually asserting the moral ideal of the wild. The spectacle, which often pits the Sherwood Outlaws against the Sheriff of Nottingham, ensures the outlaw is the moral victor, ritually asserting the people's justice over the Crown's law.

Sherwood Forest and its surrounding villages are an unparalleled global touchstone. They prove that the most durable parts of English heritage are the stories we choose to preserve, anchored to specific, ordinary

# SHERWOOD FOREST: THE MAJOR OAK

# EDWINSTOWE: MARRIAGE & THE LEGEND'S HOME

places, empowering the global family with the defiant, shared memory of justice and freedom.

## The Sublime Contrast: Sherwood's Moral Height vs. The Lake District's Aesthetic

The term sublime—an overwhelming feeling of awe and terror inspired by vastness and power—applies differently to the various "sacred" landscapes of England. While the Lake District derives its power from its physical grandeur, Sherwood Forest's sublime nature is entirely derived from its moral and legal context.

### Feature
- The Lake District (Romantic Sublime)
- Sherwood Forest (Moral Sublime)

### Source of Power
- Physical Geography (Mountains, immense scale, dramatic weather).
- Legal Geography (The punitive reach of the Forest Law and the King's authority).

### The Awe/Terror
- Awe of Nature: Fear of being lost, isolated, or overwhelmed by geological power (Wordsworthian tradition).
- Fear of Injustice: Terror of starvation, oppression, and the death penalty for hunting deer (Norman Law).

### Human Response
- Contemplation and Escapism: Humanity seeks spiritual solace by withdrawing from civilization into nature.
- Action and Defiance: Humanity is forced to act against the law to survive and assert social justice.

### The Definition of Freedom
- Natural Freedom: The freedom of a solitary individual to feel detached from social constraint.
- Communal Freedom: The freedom of the collective (The Common) to demand equity within society.

### The Result
- Aesthetic Appreciation: The landscape inspires art, poetry, and a romantic ideal of wildness.
- Ethical Imperative: The landscape inspires reclamation rituals and a continuous demand for justice.

## The Sublime Contrast: Sherwood's Moral Height vs. The Lake District's Aesthetic

The concept of the "sublime" — that overwhelming feeling of awe and terror inspired by vastness and power — manifests in profoundly different ways across England's most revered landscapes. While the Lake District draws its immense power from its physical grandeur, Sherwood Forest's sublime nature is rooted entirely in its moral and legal context.

**In the Lake District, the sublime is deeply Romantic.** Its power emanates from its sheer physical geography: towering mountains, immense scale, and dramatic weather patterns. Here, awe is born from the majesty of nature itself – a fear of being lost, isolated, or utterly overwhelmed by geological might, as famously articulated by Wordsworth. Humanity's response is one of contemplation and escapism, seeking spiritual solace by withdrawing from the clamor of civilization into the wild embrace of nature. This defines freedom as a natural, solitary state, where the individual feels detached from social constraint. The ultimate result is profound aesthetic appreciation, inspiring art, poetry, and a romantic ideal of wildness that endures to this day.

**Contrast this with Sherwood Forest, where the sublime is unequivocally moral.** Its power is derived not from natural features, but from its severe legal geography: the punitive reach of the Forest Law and the absolute authority of the King. Here, terror is not of nature, but of injustice – the crushing fear of starvation, oppression, and the brutal death penalty for the simple act of hunting a deer. Humanity's response in this environment is one of action and defiance, forced to act against an unjust law purely for survival and to assert social justice. This defines freedom not as a solitary escape, but as communal freedom – the collective (the Common) demanding equity within society. The landscape, therefore, does not primarily inspire aesthetic beauty, but rather an ethical imperative, sparking reclamation rituals and a continuous demand for justice against overbearing authority.

**Thus, two landscapes, both deemed sublime, offer antithetical lessons: one calls us to solitary wonder, the other to collective action; one to art, the other to justice.**

# HONOURING APPLIED CRAFT

THE THATCHER | DRY STONE WALLER | THE TRADITIONAL CARPENTER

# Chapter 6. Navigating Modernity: The Assault on Irreplaceable Culture

The unique, visible, and viable identity of the English village is under siege from forces that erode the cultural sovereignty once built by the Quiet Craft tradition. This is an active threat against a vital global archive, manifesting as a destructive homogenization that must be violently resisted.

1. **The Pressure of Displacement (The Demographic Trap):** We must reject the idea that our cultural jewels should be diluted by transient populations and external demographics. When the fundamental social contract of a community—the Heartbeat of the Common and the enduring social friction of the Pub and the Parish—is overwhelmed by populations detached from the local vernacular, the community's ability to act as a cultural archive is broken. This displacement is a betrayal of the past and a robbery of the future. We demand that the Enduring Community—the residents and families committed to the vernacular—supersede the needs of external volatility.
2. **The Erosion of Vernacular Skill: The Collapse of the Pact:** We should never tolerate the slow murder of self-sufficiency. When new housing utilizes generic, cheap materials, the Stonemason is replaced by the standardized brick layer. This breaks the fundamental pact between the local geology and the built environment, leading to an incremental, cowardly loss of the unique, defiant aesthetic that defines the English space. The refusal to employ local skill is a betrayal of our own land and a rejection of its embedded wisdom.

# The Global Mandate: Englishness as Essential Human Code

The survival of this culture is not a matter of local pride; it is an irreplaceable necessity for humanity. The English character, forged in the tension between the domestic and the wild, harbors a code of ethics and equity that is globally vital.

1.  **The Code of Equity and Defiance:** In the moral wilderness of Sherwood Forest, Englishness enshrined the principle that justice and equity must never be separated from law. This defiant assertion—that the common person has the moral right to correct tyranny—is a pillar of global democratic thought. The village, with its Pound Keeper and its Blacksmiths, is the physical proof that true morality rests with the common craftsman.

2.  **The Wisdom of the Common:** The Quiet Craft tradition proves that the highest forms of civilization are durable, locally sourced, and inherently resilient. The Embodied Knowledge of the Thatcher, the Wheelwright, and the Hedgerow Master offers a counter-narrative to globalized fragility—a profound lesson in local self-sovereignty that the world must preserve to teach future generations how to endure.

3.  **The Uniqueness of Place:** The fusion of architecture and locale—the honey-coloured stone, the longbow's yew, the communal oven—creates a visible, viable, and unique cultural matrix that cannot be replicated. When this singular pattern is broken, the wisdom it holds is lost forever, weakening the entire human cultural archive.

# A Defiant Act of Preservation: Reclaiming the Vernacular

Preserving the past is not about freezing it; it is about recognizing the defiant intelligence embedded in the vernacular and building the future around its immutable lessons.

1. **Honouring Applied Craft:** The future of English identity rests on reviving and respecting the trades of our ancestors. Organizations that support the Thatcher, the Dry Stone Waller, and the traditional Carpenter are not engaging in charity—they are training the next generation of cultural combatants. They prove that the most beautiful, durable, and sustainable solutions always come from the local material and the hands that possess Embodied Knowledge. This is the only path to genuine, hard-won resilience.

2. **Embracing Contradiction:** We recognize and celebrate that the most resilient villages are those that embrace their own complexity. They hold the spiritual weight of the church alongside the boisterous democracy of the pub; the ordered domesticity of the cottage alongside the moral wildness of the legend. This ability to hold contrasting, yet true, narratives is the secret of their enduring stability. This complexity is our strength; we will not surrender it for simple narratives.

The English village is a mandate. By learning to read its landscapes and honour its traditions, we cultivate a quiet competence and ensure that the Enduring Tapestry of Englishness remains not only whole, but defiantly, uniquely, and essentially human for the generations yet to come.

# THE ENDURING VILLAGE:
## HARMONY & HERITAGE

## FAMILY, TRADITION, & SKILLED GENERATIONS

The greatest existential threat to the unique, visible, and viable identity of the English village is the loss of its coherent cultural center. This is not merely an aesthetic challenge; it is a spiritual destabilization.

This crisis is driven by external forces and transient economies that sever the necessary link between a populace and the local self-sovereignty of its place. The source material asserts that when the local economy fails to sustain the Blacksmith and the Baker, the community loses its Heartbeat of the Common and its ability to organically enforce its moral code. Consequently, the built environment—the stone, the timber, the thatch— is reduced to a mere backdrop for consumption, rather than remaining an active archive of inherited wisdom. This detachment from the vernacular is identified as the core mechanism of cultural destruction.

The assertion of this culture's value lies in its durability and its potential as a global template for endurance. The sources charge the global English-speaking diaspora with Imaginative Stewardship, meaning they cannot physically preserve the architecture, but they are empowered to carry the irreplaceable code perfected in these spaces, using it as a high-fidelity cultural compass.

This meditation on the structural ingenuity and moral history of English towns and villages yields the **Seven Cornerstones of Englishness**— essential wisdom for human endurance:

**1. Practicality and Applied Craft:** The knowledge that the highest forms of civilization are durable, locally sourced, and inherently resilient. The embodied skill of the Thatcher and the Stonemason teaches that solutions rooted in local material and the skilled hand are superior to globalized, fragile convenience.

**2. Understanding Place:** The imperative to root existence in the specifics of the locale—its geology, its climate, and its resources. This wisdom must be expressed through the vernacular language and the built environment, teaching fidelity to land.

**3. Community as Moral Center:** The assertion that true morality resides not in distant centralized power, but in the binding social contract of the Heartbeat of the Common (the Pub, the Parish, the field), which is the source of local self-sovereignty.

**4. The Balance of Life:** The hard-won cultural ideal of balancing Work, Religion, and Play—from the demanding labor of the harvest to the spiritual anchor of the church, and the communal release of the May Day or Pub. This balance proves that well-being is a structural goal.

**5. Endurance and the Long View:** The lesson that cultural survival is a long-term project, gleaned from the slow, incremental evolution of villages. The ability of monuments like the Major Oak and the stone church to defy centuries of change teaches that permanence is achieved through resilience, not revolution.

**6. The Shared Language and Identity:** The collective vocabulary that allowed the English to map their world through a shared, specific lens (the shire, the moor, the down) creates a cohesive cultural matrix that enables communal action and shared moral narratives.

**7. Peaceful Domesticity:** The core, enduring cultural ideal, often expressed as the dream of "Merry England," which defines the emotional goal toward which justice and resilience strive.

By maintaining the physical landscape, the skills, and the moral narratives of the English town and village, we ensure that a crucial and brilliant code for humanity's survival endures. This is the Enduring Power of Connection to Place as exemplified by the English village.

Foundational Texts & Resources for the English Vernacular

## I. The Wisdom of Applied Craft & Place

1. The Pattern of English Building by Alec Clifton-Taylor: A seminal 1972 work (revised editions available) on regional building materials and architecture, praised for its detailed mapping of geology to built environments like Cotswold stone.
2. The Old Ways: A Journey on Foot by Robert Macfarlane: A 2012 bestseller exploring ancient paths and human-landscape interactions, with over 11,000 Goodreads ratings and widespread acclaim as a modern classic on place.
3. The Unwritten Laws of the Village (Various Medieval Texts compiled by historians): Not verified as a specific compilation. No direct academic collection matches this title. However, related concepts appear in folklore studies on medieval village customs (e.g., manorial records and customary law in works like those from the Selden Society). For authenticity, consider Customary Law in the Village excerpts in broader medieval legal histories.
4. The Woodwright's Shop by Roy Underhill: A 1981 guide (with ongoing PBS series tie-in) to traditional woodworking, emphasizing hand tools and timber mastery—ideal for understanding vernacular craft skills.
5. A History of Farm Buildings in England and Wales by Nigel Harvey: A 1970 classic (reprinted 1984) detailing agrarian architecture like cruck barns, confirming the engineering of necessity in rural structures.

## II. Social Fabric, Justice, and Domestic Balance
1. The English Village by Richard Muir: A 1980 illustrated history of village formation, economics, and communal life, blending topography with social analysis.
2. The Making of the English Working Class by E.P. Thompson: The 1963 magnum opus on social resistance and class formation (1790–1832), foundational for understanding moral justice and Sherwood-inspired myths.

3. Traditional English Customs and Festivals by Christina Hole: Verified real (exact title: English Traditional Customs, 1975). Covers festivals like May Day, blending pagan-Christian elements for insights into life's balance.
4. The Ballads of Robin Hood (Various Academic Collections): Early ballads (e.g., 15th–16th century) compiled in scholarly editions like The Ballads of Robin Hood (1977 Limited Editions Club) or Project Gutenberg's English/Scottish collections, emphasizing tradesmen over nobility.
5. The Medieval Vintners, Bakers, and Brewers of London (Academic Studies): Not verified as a specific title. No matching book found. Related authentic works include dissertations like Change is Brewing: The Industrialization of the London Beer-Brewing Trade, 1400–1750 (2014) or guild studies in Medieval Londoners resources, covering trade regulations and economic sovereignty.

III. Modern Cultural Compass & Continuity
1. English Heritage (Official Guides and Publications): The UK's leading heritage organization offers verified guides to sites like historic farms and castles, with a dedicated shop for books anchoring shared identity.
2. The Idea of a Regional Landscape: Studies in Englishness by Stephen Daniels: Not verified as a specific title. No matching book. Daniels' real work Fields of Vision: Landscape Imagery and National Identity in England and the United States (1993) closely aligns, exploring regional identity construction in places like the Cotswolds.
3. The Shell Book of English Villages by John Hadfield: A 1980 illustrated survey (edited by Hadfield) celebrating regional village styles and domesticity.
4. The Enduring Stone: Vernacular Architecture in the Cotswolds (Regional Studies): Not verified as a specific title. No matching book. Authentic alternatives include Cotswold Architecture studies (e.g., Historic England's guides) or The Cotswolds features in Traditional Building Magazine, applying geology pacts to regional endurance.
5. Local History and Folklore Societies (Online Archives): Numerous UK groups like the British Association for Local History (BALH), Folklore Society Library at UCL, and British Online Archives provide granular parish records, oral traditions, and disputes for community-centered endurance.

www.ingramcontent.com/pod-product-compliance
Lightning Source LLC
Chambersburg PA
CBHW020808130626
46554CB00006B/2327